T0199143

OTHER BOOKS BY THIS AUTHOR:

The Christmas Story
Step into Scripture
A Bible Study for Advent

The Book on Bullies:
How to Handle Them without Becoming One of Them

The Book on Bullies: Break Free in
Forty (40 Minutes or 40 Days)
Includes 40 Devotionals to Fortify Your Soul

SEDER TO SUNDAY STEP INTO SCRIPTURE

A BIBLE STUDY FOR EASTER

SUSAN K. BOYD

WESTBOW
P R E S S®
A DIVISION OF THOMAS NELSON
& ZONDERVAN

All Scripture quotations, unless otherwise indicated, are taken from the Holy
Bible, New International Version®, NIV®. Copyright ©1973, 1978, 1984, 2011 by
Biblica, Inc.™ Used by permission of Zondervan. All rights reserved worldwide.
www.zondervan.com The "NIV" and "New International Version" are trademarks
registered in the United States Patent and Trademark Office by Biblica, Inc.™

Scripture taken from the New King James Version®. Copyright © 1982
by Thomas Nelson. Used by permission. All rights reserved.

WestBow Press books may be ordered through booksellers or by contacting:

WestBow Press
A Division of Thomas Nelson & Zondervan
1663 Liberty Drive
Bloomington, IN 47403
www.westbowpress.com
1 (866) 928-1240

www.sedertosunday.com

ISBN: 978-1-9736-3837-7 (sc)
ISBN: 978-1-9736-3838-4 (hc)
ISBN: 978-1-9736-3836-0 (e)

Library of Congress Control Number: 2018910257

Print information available on the last page.

WestBow Press rev. date: 09/18/2019

To my dear son: I love you and am so thankful for you! I admire your strong faith and the way you love God and his Scripture. I pray God blesses your children and someday their children as they enjoy the adventure of studying God's Word and sharing his love with others!

SEDER TO SUNDAY PREVIEW

Seder

I watched you kneel before Judas,
His filthy feet in your hands.
"You're not all clean," you spoke of his heart,
But he refused to understand.

Gethsemane

You stepped up to the soldiers.
"I AM he," you made yourself known.
We fought for you in the garden,
But then we left you all alone.

Trial and Crucifixion

You stood innocent before Pilate.
I heard the crowd shout, "Crucify!"
All of our hopes were nailed to your cross
The day we watched you die.

Easter Sunday

You rose while we were sleeping.
Then we saw you everywhere,
On the road to Emmaus and in a room.
The tomb? You're no longer there!

CONTENTS

PREFACE

When I was young watching epic movies at the Fox Theater, I didn't simply sink back into my chair as a spectator; I felt like I stepped into the picture and onto the screen. When Moses (Charlton Heston) led a million people out of Egypt while being chased by Pharaoh (Yul Brenner) and his soldiers in chariots, I was there. When Moses raised his arms in prayer and the Red Sea miraculously parted, I was there too! I wondered what it would be like to step between two enormous walls of water armed with nothing but my faith. I have great memories of those afternoons when I joined the characters on the wide screen in all their circumstances.

Today, people get help interacting with movie plots. IMAX theaters move viewers into the picture. 3-D movies transport the picture out to the audience. Home theaters bring the movie atmosphere to where people live. And most interactive of all are the video and virtual reality games. They feature the players as the stars of the show, placing them in the middle of all the action.

Whether playing a game or watching others on

the big screen, many want to participate. I understand that feeling. I was engaged in every way possible in the sights, sounds, and stories of the people I wanted to see. As a child, I tried to find the seat that would allow me the best view of the movie. I still do this; maybe you do too.

The cinema experience was the inspiration for creating *Seder to Sunday: Step into Scripture, a Bible Study for Easter*. This book is the first in the *Step into Scripture* Bible study series. This is your opportunity to view biblical events as an epic film and to step into any scene as an active participant.

Scripture is the script! It describes a drama filled with moral struggles, betrayal, friendships, villains, and undying hope. It is also evidence of the supernatural with all the special effects. Best of all, Scripture is a true story of eternal devotion in which God makes the ultimate sacrifice for those he loves.

As you begin this study, you will be opening a hole in time through which you can travel to biblical and historical settings. Then, stepping back to today, you can apply what you learned. You will use your imagination, but the good news is that you don't need much of it! The scenery will be painted, the stage set with characters in place.

The Bible study is the director, suggesting thoughts or feelings your character might have. You, however, make the final decision about what you think, feel, or do in any situation. The study is just here to assist you. Best of all, no answer is considered wrong when based on Scripture. Your perspective is what makes *Seder to Sunday* come to life!

You may want to use this study for a few days or weeks. This can be a family or a group Bible study or your private journey with Christ. Whether you watch the events from afar or insert yourself into the story, you will determine the impact these verses will have on you.

The Old Testament passages offer prophecies pointing to the Messiah. The four gospels are rich in teachings, miracles, and events from the life of Christ. Reading about these few days can become more than simply an intellectual study. It can be an experience of Christ, close up and personal, from Seder to Sunday.

INTRODUCTION

Two Reasons to Choose This Bible Study

The first reason to use this study is to step into Scripture. This will allow you to come alongside Jesus and the people who were with him and to be present at the important events in history. These scenes are not author's plots or story lines. They are the facts according to the four gospels. Though the study is interactive, it does not alter the facts but freely uses historical sources to create a vivid and realistic setting for those facts.

This is a new and different style of study, intended to move you the way people who walked with Jesus were moved by his life. This type of interactive Bible study is not in any way meant to replace the traditional approach to studying the Bible. It would not work easily for most biblical stories. It does, however, lend itself in an exciting way to the events from Seder to Sunday.

The second reason to choose this study is to learn the truth about what happened from Seder to Sunday. Comparing all the Gospels and using research by archaeologists and historians along with accounts by contemporaries of Jesus, we have more than enough evidence to prove the accuracy of events depicted in Scripture. The Bible gives us an awe-inspiring record we can experience and believe.

How to Use This Bible Study

Read each scene and question aloud. Imagine you are watching and listening to a movie. Try to resist the temptation to skip over a scene or a question, as that would be like going for popcorn in the middle of a movie and then asking the person next to you what you missed! This is a movie with you in it. Freeze the picture in your mind as you look up Scripture.

You can find all your answers from verses within the question. If you are interested in additional verses, use the Scripture passages under the lesson heading at the top of the page.

Some of the questions will ask what you are doing, thinking, or feeling during a scene. Whatever you experience as you step into Scripture is the right answer for each question.

Occasionally, you will see the heading "Note" which takes you behind the scenes. A note may offer historical background or additional information, giving you a context for a verse or a question. A section labeled "Scene" describes the picture you are seeing and where you are at that time. If you are in a group study, be sure to read the scenes aloud so you all see the same picture you would see if you were sitting in a theater watching a movie together. (Scripture citations will be provided frequently so you can find a scene in the Bible.)

The more you invest yourself in each question and scene, staying involved with the people and the action, the more you will get out of *Seder to Sunday*. Try to avoid stepping back to analyze. Instead step up and take part. Scripture supplies the inspirational Word, and the Holy Spirit guides your unique personal insight. Step into the pages of your Bible and discover a world that may change yours forever.

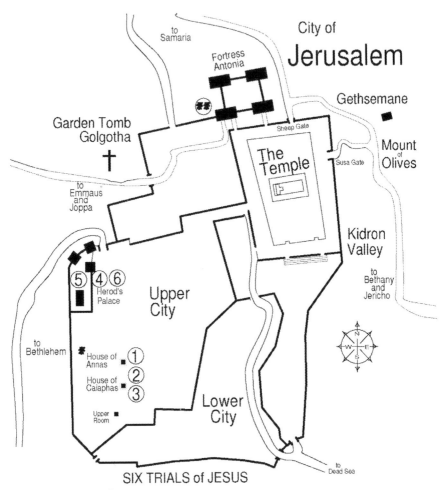

to Samaria

City of **Jerusalem**

Fortress Antonia

Gethsemane

Garden Tomb Golgotha

Sheep Gate

The Temple

Susa Gate

Mount of Olives

to Emmaus and Joppa

Kidron Valley

to Bethany and Jericho

⑤ ④ ⑥ Herod's Palace

Upper City

to Bethlehem

House of Annas ①

House of Caiaphas ② ③

Upper Room

Lower City

to Dead Sea

N W E S

SIX TRIALS of JESUS

① Interrogation by Annas
② Interrogation by Caiaphas
③ Trial by Caiaphas & Sanhedrin
④ Hearing by Pilate
⑤ Trial by Herod
⑥ Trial by Pilate

✳ Possible house of Annas   ✳✳ Possible trial by Pilate

SEDER DINNER: CELEBRATING PASSOVER

MATTHEW 26:17–19; MARK 14:12–16; LUKE 22:1–20

Note

The sequence of events in each gospel as well as the content may vary, depending on where each author puts his emphasis. This study will keep a flow, using the Gospels to present a full picture of the life of Jesus from Seder to Sunday.

Scene

You walk up steps to a second-story room and push open the door. This is where you will share Passover dinner tonight with your rabbi, Jesus, and with the other disciples. All you can think about are the experiences of recent weeks, especially hearing the crowds shouting for Jesus as he entered Jerusalem. The whole world seems to chase after Jesus of Nazareth, your friend and teacher!

Your fellow Jews shouted "Hosanna," taking off their coats and tearing branches off date palms to place them in the path of the donkey as Jesus rode through Jerusalem.[1] They treated him as if he were a prophet, or perhaps a king, entering the great city (Mark 11:1–10; Luke 19:28–40; John 12:12–19)! Even travelers making their annual pilgrimages to the city for Passover waved palm branches and called out to him as he rode by.

You laughed at the dignified chief priests frantically waving their arms in protest, demanding Jesus tell the people to stop their adoration of him. Jesus never flinched. His only comment: "If they keep quiet the stones will cry out" (Luke 19:40).

Everyone knew Annas (the high priest emeritus) and the other religious rulers were angry with Jesus. You recall the day Jesus cleared out the temple. He chased out the sacrificial animals and turned over the tables of the greedy money changers (John 2:15). You imagine how that cut into the profits of Annas!

Annas, the power behind the chief priests, was thought to have made money on the inflated rate of exchange for currency at the temple. He also was suspected of profiting by demanding that worshippers buy the temple animals rather than bring their own for sacrifice. The priests often rejected a person's animal, frequently finding a blemish or defect. The business of buying and selling in the temple was well known by all the people, as the Bazaar of Annas.[2]

The religious aristocracy became more enraged when Jesus cleared out the temple a second time. He did this following his triumphant entry into Jerusalem. After again turning over tables and driving out money changers, Jesus announced so Annas and all his contracted thieves could hear, "My Father's house is a house of prayer and you have made it a den of robbers!" (Matthew 21:12–13).

You and the other disciples are worried your teacher is making enemies in high places, but you are proud of him for being a friend to those in the lowest places (John 8:59; John 11:8).

Working alongside Jesus and listening to his teaching these three and a half years has been exciting.[3] You are continually surprised by his miraculous powers. His fame has grown to the point that he is now known throughout the country as a "wise man and doer of wonderful works."[4] He heals the sick, raises the dead, and quiets the waves on Lake Galilee with but a word!

As you think back to that frenzied crowd making a narrow path for Jesus to ride triumphantly through the streets of Jerusalem, you recall how Roman soldiers simply stood back to watch. You believe Jesus to be the Messiah. What better time than now at Passover for him to lead his people out from under the heel of Roman occupation? You are ready to assume responsibility at his side whenever he declares his kingdom. Now, more than ever, you and the other disciples believe his rightful place is to be king of the Jews (Zechariah 9:9–10; Isaiah 9:6-7; John 1:41).

You and your friends recline on comfortable pillows around a long, U-shaped table. This is an important holiday commemorating the Jews' freedom from their bondage in Egypt. Tonight you will eat and share with Jesus in the Passover or Seder dinner. (Note: *Seder* means a set order. Each part of the meal has significance, looking back to the first Passover and to God's provision for the salvation of his people. The ritual meal is celebrated as a family or, in this case, by friends who have become as close as family.)

1. Jesus puts you next to him and looks you in the eye, saying, "I have eagerly looked forward to eating this Passover dinner with you, _____, before I suffer." (Write your name in the blank and say this statement out loud; see also Luke 22:14–16.) Are you surprised you are this important to him?

2. Will you wait for Jesus to speak, or do you want to ask him to explain what he means by "suffer"?

3. First you should read Exodus 12:1–30 to understand the reason for the Passover dinner. How does Jesus seem to be linking the historical Passover in Egypt to this night's dinner (Exodus 12:21-27; Matthew 26:26–29; Luke 22:14–20)? Before you answer, remember when you walked by the sea with John the Baptist and he first pointed out Jesus to you (John 1:29).

4. **Step out of Scripture and back to today for this question.** Israelites in Egypt obediently applied the blood of the lamb over their doorways, and death passed over them. All those in each household survived solely because they were under the protection of the blood. This also symbolized a future time when death would pass over all believers in Jesus, "the Lamb of God," whose shed blood made possible eternal life (Romans 5:9; Hebrews 2:9, 10:10). Is this confusing or comforting to you today?

5. Jesus now does something that is a complete departure from a Seder meal. He tears off pieces of bread and gives them to all of you! Nothing is to be eaten once the Passover meal is finished.[5] All the disciples, including you, know that. The lamb and the other parts of the meal have been eaten. The bread and the cups of wine that are part of the Seder dinner ceremony also are finished. Jesus

now declares this bread he gives everyone to be his body given for you (Luke 22:19–20). This last cup of wine he proclaims to be his blood poured out for you. What is he saying about himself?

6. You think back to another time when you heard Jesus say, in public, that his body was the bread that came down from heaven. Sadly, many of his closest followers became confused by those words; they turned away from him after that (John 6:47–68). What are you remembering? What do you imagine he means by all of this?

7. **Step out of Scripture and back to today for this question. This is a four-part question.** Make a list of people you would possibly rescue in a life-threatening situation even if it meant giving up your own life. Examples could be family or friends. List people or those committing certain types of crimes you might not risk your life to save. Why do you think Jesus planned to die for the sins of everyone, knowing some would love him back and others would be apathetic or antagonistic toward him? What does John 3:16-17 say about God's purpose and our response?

THE LAST SUPPER
(EXODUS 12:21–25; JOHN 1:29)

A Passover meal of longing
For your disciples to understand.
A cross, a cost, as in Egypt.
Now you are the Passover lamb.

BAD NEWS: BETRAYAL

MATTHEW 26:20–25; MARK 14:18–21;
LUKE 22:21–23; JOHN 13:18–30

Scene

Jesus, in the previous lesson, shared shocking news about what was going to happen to him. He now hands out pieces of bread, telling you something unbelievable—that you or one of your friends in this room will soon betray him.

1. What questions are your friends asking (Mark 14:18–19; Luke 22:21–23; John 13:21–25)? Many Bible scholars believe "the disciple whom Jesus loved" was possibly John, since John was the author of the gospel where this phrase appears.[1] This does not mean Jesus loved the others less. John may have felt confident in the loving relationship he

enjoyed with Jesus, declaring this throughout these passages without divulging his own name.

2. How does Jesus try to warn Judas that he knows what Judas has done and is about to do (Matthew 26:23–25; Luke 22:21–22)?

3. Jesus knows the past and the future. What does Jesus know has happened these last weeks and will happen moments from now? To see the full picture, read these passages: Matthew 26:14–16; John 12:4–6, 13:26–27, 30.

4. What are you thinking of doing if Jesus tells you the name of his betrayer? Do you wonder if you could ever be his betrayer?

5. **Step out of Scripture, back to today for this question. This is a three-part question.** Prophetic Scripture passages told of a betrayer (Psalm 41:9). Did the betrayer have to be Judas? (This has been debated through the ages so if you are discussing this in a group, give each other lots of room for difference of opinion.) When, have you in the past planned to do something you later regretted? How do you think staying close to Jesus and talking it over with him could have made a difference for you?

BACK FROM BETRAYAL

(JOHN 12:3-8; MATTHEW 26:14-16; JOHN 13:21-30)

Lord, is anything more important than you?
What would thirty pieces of silver do?
Would it soothe greed, disappointment, or pride?
Create a rationale to justify or hide?

Small decisions made every day
Bring me closer or pull me further away
From the Savior I've come to know,
And so …

Tonight when I'm tempted to go
"Quickly do" what you already know,
I'll sit beside you; you'll smile if I say,
"My heart tells me to stay."

MATTHEW, 27.

A. D. 33.

¶ ch. 26, 63.
John 19. 10.

crucified him, and parted his garments, casting lots: that it might be fulfilled which was spoken by the prophet, "They parted my garments among them, and upon my vesture did they cast lots.

35 And they crucified him, and parted his garments, casting lots: that it might be fulfilled which was spoken by the prophet, "They parted my garments among them, and upon my vesture did they cast lots.

36 And sitting down they watched him there;

37 And set up over his head his accusation written, THIS IS JESUS THE KING OF THE JEWS.

38 Then were there two thieves crucified with him, one on the right hand, and another on the left.

39 ¶ And "they that passed by reviled him, wagging their heads,

40 And saying, "Thou that destroyest the temple, and buildest it in three days, save thyself. If thou be the Son of God, come down from the cross.

41 Likewise also the chief priests mocking him, with the scribes and elders, said,

42 He saved others; himself he cannot save. If he be the King of Israel, let him now come down from the cross, and we will believe him.

43 He "trusted in God; let him deliver him now, if he will have him: for he said, I am the Son of God.

44 The "thieves also, which were crucified with him, cast the same in his teeth.

45 Now "from the sixth hour there was darkness over all the land unto the ninth hour.

46 And about the ninth hour Jesus cried with a loud voice, saying, E'lī, E'lī, lā'mā sā-bāch'thā-nī? that is to say, "My God, my God, why hast thou forsaken me?

47 Some of them that stood there, when they heard that, said, This man calleth for E-lī'as.

48 And straightway one of them ran, and took a spunge, and filled it with vinegar, and put it on a reed, and gave him to drink.

49 The rest said, Let be, let us see whether E-lī'as will come to save him.

50 ¶ Jesus, when he had cried again with a

LESSON 3

WHO IS THE GREATEST?

MATTHEW 26:18–29; MARK 14:12–25;
LUKE: 22:23–30; JOHN 13-17

Note

A little clarification is needed to understand the possible meaning of John 13:1, which says this night is "just before the Passover festival." The seven days following the Passover meal were known as the Feast of Unleavened Bread. This was also called the Passover (Luke 22:1).

John and Luke's gospels work well together to set the stage for this scene at the Seder dinner. They offer information not found in the books of Matthew and Mark. (All relevant gospel passages are listed at the top of the page for easy reference.)

Luke covers the dispute the disciples have about greatness. This dispute was possibly the result of their ambition to stand out and to be chosen for Jesus's cabinet, with the expectation of his coming to power. By contrast, John focuses on service, humility, and heart cleansing (by the washing of the disciples' feet) and recounts Jesus's prayer for his own.

1. This is a three-part question. What is the new topic of conversation between you and your friends at the Passover dinner (Luke 22:24)? What does Jesus say about greatness (Luke 22:25–27)? Describe the position of leadership and of responsibility Jesus promises the disciples will have someday in the kingdom of God (Luke 22:28–30).

2. How does Jesus handle this dispute about greatness and leadership in washing the feet of all of his disciples (John 13:3–5)? (Note: The streets of Palestine were dusty, and it was a common courtesy for a host to have a servant wash the feet of his guests.[1] A plan had apparently not been made for washing feet. No servant was hired to do this. None of the disciples moved to wash one another's feet or even the feet of their teacher.)

3. Are you, like Peter, embarrassed to see Jesus on the ground holding your filthy feet in his hands (John 13:5)?

4. Is this your view of leadership? If not, describe how you define it?

5. How does this act of humility and of great love differ from the world's view of greatness (John 13:12–17)?

6. **Step out of Scripture and back to today for this question.** Give current examples of the world's idea of greatness.

7. Why do you think Jesus is washing everyone's feet (John 13:10–17)? Describe the expression you see on the face of Judas as Jesus washes and dries his feet. No one else but you notices this (John 13:10–11).

8. What do you want to say to Jesus as he pours water over your feet, or do you just want him to finish?

9. Is Peter loud and indignant when he protests, or is he bending down, quietly pleading (John 13:5–10)? What do you hear? What do you see?

Scene

Jesus returns to the table and sits down. He continues to speak. He tears off pieces of the unleavened bread, preparing to hand these to you and to the other disciples. You do not hear everything your rabbi says, because your friends are speculating about the identity of the betrayer. Each declares his allegiance to Jesus.

Jesus appears to give special honor to one of the disciples by tearing off the first piece of bread, dipping it, and handing it to him. You wonder what Judas has done to deserve this attention. You think maybe this is because he is the treasurer and Jesus entrusts him with so much. Then Jesus tells Judas, "What you are about to do, do quickly" (John 13:26–30).

Judas abruptly leaves. You assume Jesus told Judas to buy more food for the festival or to give money to the poor. You think, *Lucky Judas to be given such trust and responsibility!* For a moment you wish you were the disciple given this honor.

After Judas leaves, Jesus shares more personal information about the future (John 13:31-16:33). Then Jesus looks upward as if he and his Heavenly Father are the only ones in the room as he begins to pray (John 17:1-5). Now he is speaking at length to his Father about you (John 17:6-26)!

10. **Step out of Scripture and back to today for an important exercise.** Insert your name in the prayer Jesus prays over you. Wherever you read the words *them*, *those*, or *they*, he is referring to you as well as to the others who sit with him at the Passover

dinner. This prayer includes everyone in each generation who follows or who will follow Jesus. By personalizing this prayer, you will know more fully how Jesus feels about you.

Note

To make this exercise easier, the prayer (John 17:6–26) is written below. You need only write your name in the first blank and then read the prayer aloud, saying your name whenever you see a blank space. The prayer is long, but try not to skip it because of the length. Jesus is speaking to his heavenly Father on your behalf! *To experience the full impact of this intimate prayer, in the silence of the moments when you are doing this study, speak your name.*

I have revealed you to _____,
whom you gave me out of the world.
_____ was yours; you gave_____ to me
and_____ obeyed your word. Now_____
knows that everything you have given me
comes from you. For I gave_____ the
words you gave me and_____ accepted

them. _____ knew, with certainty, that I came from you, and_____ believed that you sent me. I pray for_____ . I am not praying for the world, but for_____ which you gave me because_____ is yours. All I have is yours and all you have is mine. And glory has come to me through_____ . I will remain in the world no longer, but_____ is still in the world, and I am coming to you. Holy Father, protect_____ by the power of your name—the name you gave me—so that_____ and other believers may be one as we are one. While I was with_____ I protected_____ and kept_____ safe by that name that you gave me. None has been lost except the one doomed to destruction, so that Scripture would be fulfilled.

I am coming to you, now, but I say these things while I am still in the world so that_____ may have the full measure of my joy. I have given_____ your word and the world has hated_____, for_____ is not of the world any more than I am of the world. My prayer is not that you take_____ out of the world but that you protect_____ from the evil one. _____

is not, of the world, even, as I am not of it. Sanctify_____ with the truth; your word is truth. As you sent me into the world I have sent_____ into the world. For_____ I sanctify myself, that_____ too may be truly sanctified. My prayer is not for_____alone. I pray also for those who will believe in me through_____ 's message, that all believers may be one, Father, just as you are in me and I am in you. May believers also be in us so that the world may believe that you have sent me. I have given_____ and other believers the glory, that you have given me that they may be one as we are one. I am in the believers and you in me.

May_____ and other believers be brought to complete unity to let the world know that you have sent me and love_____ and other believers, even as you have loved me. Father, I want_____ whom you have given me, to be with me where I am, and to see my glory, the glory you have given me because you loved me, before the creation of the world. Righteous Father, though the world does not know you, I know you and_____ knows that you have sent me. I have made

you known to _____, and will continue
to make you known in order that the love
you have for me may be in_____ and
that I myself may be in_____ .

11. **Step out of Scripture and back to today for this question. This is a three-part question.** Is Jesus's prayer for his own more meaningful to you after inserting your name? Which phrase had an impact on you? Why?

DIRTY FEET

Lord, my feet got dirty
Where I walked today.
I stepped in some of the selfish places
That were so familiar along the way.

I thought the road was cleared
And my self-centeredness was gone.
Then everywhere I put my foot,
I found I was dragging it along.

Like particles of dust
That I don't quite see are there,
I hadn't noticed a clinging self-pity
Until I tried to shake off despair.

There is no water or towel
To wash me clean and new,
Only a Savior who poured out his life,
Cleansing me through and through.

Lord, change my route of travel.
My feet got dirty where I walked today.
Thank you, Lord, for what your forgiveness
Alone can wash away.

LESSON 4

PRAYER AND PREPARATION IN THE GARDEN

MATTHEW 26:30-45; MARK 14:26-42;
LUKE 22:31-46; JOHN 18:1

Scene

After the Passover dinner Jesus leads you in singing a hymn (Matthew 26:30). You and your friends step down the stairs and outside. Together you walk through the countryside, across the Kidron Valley, and up to the Mount of Olives. You follow Jesus, talking and occasionally looking back in the distance on thousands of tents sheltering pilgrims who came to celebrate Passover. You all go to a familiar secluded place called Gethsemane, on the lower slopes of the Mount of Olives.

You have gone to this quiet garden retreat together many other evenings to pray and to finish your day worshipping God. This is a peaceful time with close friends, away from crowds and people's demands.

Arriving at the garden, you stop and stand among the olive trees. Jesus turns to you and the others. In a soft, sad voice, he says that tonight you will all run away and leave him alone (Matthew 26:31-35; Luke 22:31-32). (Note: This may be a fulfillment of a prophecy in Zechariah 13:7.)

1. How has the mood changed?

2. Peter is protesting again tonight. He believes he knows himself better than Jesus knows him. Explain Peter's argument with Jesus (Matthew 26:33–35).

3. Is Peter the only one vowing his loyalty (Mark 14:27–31)?

4. What are you saying to Jesus?

Note

Jesus devotes most of his time in the garden to prayer. This is his preparation for the terrible events to come. This is your preparation as well.

5. Do you want to sit and wait with most of the disciples or be one of the chosen men Jesus takes deeper into the garden (Matthew 26:36–45)?

6. What personal information does Jesus share with you, James, John, and Peter (Matthew 26:36–38)?

7. Why does Jesus keep returning to you (Matthew 26:40–41)?

8. What is making you so tired (Matthew 26:41)? Do you feel overwhelmed and depressed by the disturbing predictions Jesus made at dinner and here in the garden? Are you just sleepy? Write out the possibilities.

9. What are you hearing Jesus pray (Mark 14:36–40)? How long does he wrestle with these issues in prayer—a few minutes or hours?

10. You cannot keep awake. What are you again hearing said (Matthew 26:42)?

11. Why does Jesus ask that you watch and pray with him (Matthew 26:38–41)? Is it because he needs prayer or because he knows you will need it? Or could it be both?

12. **Step out of Scripture and back to today for this question. This is a two-part question.** Have you been struggling with a decision in your life lately? Do you find comfort knowing God's Son struggled before coming to his decision, "nevertheless, not my will, but yours, be done" (Luke 22:42 NKJV)?

YOUR WILL

You prepared for the cross in the garden
And my salvation before time.
Prepare my heart to find the courage
To do your will, not mine.

THE TRAITOR'S KISS AND THE SAVIOR'S SWORD

MATTHEW 26:14-16, 46-56; MARK 14:42-52;
LUKE 22:1-6, 47-54; JOHN 18:1-12

Note

If you desire more behind-the-scenes information and additional dialogue in the garden, refer to the above verses.

Scene

You feel a hand on your shoulder gently waking you. You cannot believe you fell asleep yet again! Jesus smiles sadly and says quietly, "Are you still sleeping and resting?"

Then he announces loudly enough for all to hear, "Look, the hour has come and the Son of Man is delivered into the hands of sinners. Rise. Let's go. Here comes my betrayer!" (Matthew 26:45–46). Jesus peers out into the garden. You notice that his hair and his garments are soaked with perspiration. He looks as if he has been laboring the whole evening. All of your friends are gathered around him now. You and the others look questioningly at Jesus and then at each other.

All at once the night is glowing with the light of torches, and you hear the sound of flames being whipped about by the evening breeze (John 18:1–12). The long shadows of invading strangers move along the olive trees. You hear the marching of soldiers and the clanking of swords at their sides. (Note: A detachment of soldiers is a cohort or one tenth of a legion, which means three hundred to six hundred soldiers are slowly entering the garden.)

Men in robes make their way through the garden, swinging clubs. You are getting nervous but you can't see any faces yet. You feel the adrenaline pumping through your veins. A man steps up to Jesus and kisses him on the cheek in a friend's greeting. Judas! Jesus asks his disciple, "Would you betray the Son of Man with a kiss?" (Luke 22:48).

1. What are you doing at this moment? Are you trying to reason with the soldiers? Are you shouting at Judas that he is a traitor? Are you trying to pull Jesus away? Are your friends ready to fight (Luke 22:49)? Peter is drawing the short sword he brought.

Scene

Jesus senses the mood in the garden as the disciples and soldiers become angry and tense. He intervenes quickly and asks, "Who is it you seek?" They say, "Jesus of Nazareth." Then in a deep, authoritative voice you have never heard before or since, Jesus declares, "I am he."

All of the soldiers, chief priests, and elders are forced to the ground (John 18:1-6). You wonder if fear or God's unseen, unheard power made their knees buckle. Jesus leaves you awestruck as he has done so many other occasions.

You recall the story of Moses meeting God in the burning bush on the mountainside (Exodus 3:10–15). God told Moses, "Go to Pharaoh and bring the Israelites out of Egypt." Moses asked for God's name, and God declared, "Tell them I AM has sent you" (Exodus 3:13–16).

You suddenly realize the same power that spoke from the burning bush to Moses long ago, the majesty of the great I AM, is standing here! You are filled with hope and courage. Maybe this is the moment you have envisioned when Jesus will take back the throne and the glory of King David! After all, the Master's enemies are on the ground and he is standing over them (John 18:4–9).

Jesus approaches the demoralized soldiers, who are trying to get to their feet. He poses his question again, as if to remind them why they have come. "Who is it you want? I told you I am he. If you are looking for me, then let these men go."

You are stunned by his words. Then Jesus's earlier prayer for you fills your mind: "While I was with them, I protected them and kept them safe by that name you gave me" (John 17:11–12). You quickly reflect back. You can hardly believe it was such a short time ago, tonight, that he prayed his protective prayer over you and your friends—his friends!

Standing over the bewildered soldiers, you and the other disciples feel bolder and shout, "Lord, should we strike with our swords?" (Luke 22:49–50). Peter does not wait for an answer. Seizing the moment, he decides to strike first to protect Jesus. With full force, Peter swings his sword, cutting off the ear of Malchus, the high priest's servant (John 18:10–11).

2. What is your initial reaction?

Scene

Jesus drops to his knees, drawing close to Malchus, who is now screaming and writhing in pain (Luke

22:51). Christ gently takes the severed ear and holds it to the man's head, miraculously reattaching it. Except for the blood around the man's face and neck and on the ground, his injury is undetectable.

3. Are you watching the healing at Christ's hands or looking at the soldiers' hands now gripping their swords?

4. What does Jesus say to Peter about his drawn sword? How many angels does Jesus say are available to defend him at this moment (Matthew 26:52–54; John 18:11)? (Note: One Roman legion has three thousand to six thousand soldiers.[1])

5. Which words of Jesus make you wonder what he knows that you don't (Matthew 26:54, 56)?

Scene

Jesus confronts his enemies, asking, "Am I leading a rebellion, that you have to come with swords and clubs? Every day I was with you in the temple courts, and you did not lay a hand on me. But this is your hour—when darkness reigns" (Luke 22:52–53).

Hearing those words, the soldiers for the first time roughly grab hold of Jesus. They wrench his arms backward, pulling his hands painfully high up between his shoulder blades. Then they tightly bind his wrists together with leather straps. They are taking him away.

A question flashes through your mind: *Jesus, what do you want me to do?* Some of the soldiers have now turned their attention to you. Fear washes over you, and you quickly consider your options. The soldiers are in a rage and are suddenly full of confidence. You are terrified and paralyzed until you think, *What good will it do Jesus if I am arrested too?*

6. What is going on inside and outside of you as you watch your once-powerful leader now look the victim (Matthew 26:56–57; Mark 14:50; Luke 22:54)?

Scene

You back up out of the garden. Turning and darting between the olive trees and down the dark hill, you see a young man also trying to get away. The soldiers catch him.

The terrified young man twists and squirms in their hands until the soldiers are left holding nothing but his garments. You see the figure running in the distance, a flicker of light from somewhere shining on his back. You wonder who he is.

As you race away, you catch a glimpse of the disciples scattering in every direction, trying to get far from Gethsemane (Mark 14: 50-52). You don't stop to look. You are running for your life!

7. Where are you going?

8. **Step out of Scripture and back to today for this question. This is a three-part question.** Have you ever felt so threatened you just wanted to escape? Describe the situation. What were you thinking and feeling and what did you do?

JESUS IN THE GARDEN

Peaceful garden, disciples around you,
You are sharing what is to come.
As torches and enemies surround you,
No friends in sight. Not one.

LESSON 6

DENIAL

MATTHEW 26:57-59, 66-75; MARK 14:53-54,
63-72; LUKE 22:54-62; JOHN 18:12-27

Scene

Finally stopping to catch your breath, you realize you have deserted Jesus. You make your way down to the town of Jerusalem. Moving carefully behind buildings, you step around a corner and see your rabbi.

You follow the soldiers from a safe distance. The streets are quiet on this late Passover night. The only sound is the awful steady marching of soldiers. You see Peter following in the shadows behind them with John (the other disciple).

1. What is Peter doing and why (Matthew 26:57–58; John 18:15–18)? (Note: Many Bible scholars have identified "the other disciple" as possibly being John.[1])

Scene

The chief priests and members of the Sanhedrin are filing into the palace where the soldiers are taking Jesus. You step into the courtyard just outside of the building where the trial begins. You pull your outer cloak up around your face and head to keep warm and hidden. You shiver in the cold night air.

You had caught up with Peter and John just as the soldiers and temple guards were taking Jesus through the courtyard gate of the high priest's palace. John knew the high priest and was immediately allowed to enter. John, in fact, walked into the courtyard with Jesus (John 18:15).

You and Peter were left to wait outside. Then the large door swung open. John, still talking with the servant girl who was given charge of the gate, let you and Peter into the courtyard (John 18:15–18).

The guards take Jesus to the palace of Annas, who had previously stood as high priest (John 18:12–13).

Note

The Jewish office of high priest was originally a lifetime position. The Romans, wanting control, changed high priests at will. Annas had previously been deposed from office by the Roman authorities. The Jews, however, continued to recognize him as their high priest.[2]

Annas, though not the current high priest, continued to influence the religious rulers. He used all his power to become the head of an empire of corruption in Jerusalem.[3] He, five of his sons, one son-in-law (Caiaphas), and a grandson held the high priest position at one time or another.[4]

Jews believed Annas and his family to be spies for the government and saw them as greedy and extremely abusive toward their own people, according to Werner Keller in his book *The Bible as History*.[5]

Scene

The homes of Annas and Caiaphas are adjacent to each other and share a courtyard.[6] The interrogation before Annas is brief (John 18:19–24). He now has Jesus taken to the palace of his son-in-law, Joseph Caiaphas, the current high priest.[7]

Note

A trial of this type would usually take place before the Sanhedrin during daylight hours in public at the temple. Apparently, selected members of the Sanhedrin who were part of the conspiracy to kill Jesus were the only ones informed of these secret proceedings (Matthew 26:3–5; John 11:47–53). Caiaphas used his palace for further interrogation. He summoned certain Sanhedrin members to his home to turn the questioning into a formal, though clandestine, trial.[8]

Scene

It is quiet out in the courtyard; you hear only the mumbling of people gathered nearby. The soldiers and servants move closer to the fire to get warm. Peter looks uneasy. He and the soldiers are almost rubbing elbows as they hold their hands over the flames.

You are feeling nervous too. Then from within the building, you hear men's voices being raised. The accusations are loud and clear. The people in the courtyard also become agitated.

2. A girl approaches Peter. Just moments ago, she had let Peter through the gate. What is she saying (Matthew 26:69)? Why would she think he is one of the disciples of Jesus (John 18:15–17)?

3. What is Peter's reply (Matthew 26:70)?

4. Where is Peter going and who speaks to him next (Matthew 26:71)?

5. You are nervous listening to what this second girl says to Peter and to others around him. What is his answer to her (Matthew 26:71–72)?

Scene

Even from a distance you can hear the sound of fists hitting your treasured friend and rabbi, Jesus. People who can see what is going on inside, relay to you that the soldiers have blindfolded him. The men inside laugh and shout, "Prophesy to us! Who hit you?"

You shudder, listening to the violent blows, the abuse, and the dull thud of Jesus's body hitting the stone pavement. The terrible taunting begins again. The people gathered by the fire are speaking loudly too. Like spectators on the outskirts of a fight, they look eager to participate.

6. One man in the crowd steps up to Peter for a closer look. The flickering flames cast an occasional flash of light across the disciple's face. The man inspecting Peter immediately recalls where he has seen him tonight. The accuser's eyes get large as he points at Peter and announces his suspicions. He seems to be a very convincing witness against Peter (John 18:26–27). Why does this man look so familiar to you?

7. The curious people are now pushing in around Peter as he moves closer to the gate. What is the crowd saying and what is his third reply? What does Peter add to his protest to make his denial more persuasive (Matthew 26:73–74)?

Scene

You look up and hold your breath for a moment as you see Jesus slowly coming down the steps with his hands tied behind his back. The guards are preparing to lead him away to yet another trial. Jesus turns around. He looks exhausted. His lip and the side of his face are swollen and bleeding, but his eyes are penetrating as he raises his head. Peter looks up and the Lord's eyes lock with his.

The crowd is hushed, and the only sound is a rooster crowing in the distance. Peter still has his hand raised in protest. Peter's hand drops to his side, and his expression turns from anger and fear to horror and sadness at the sight of his teacher and friend.

The crowd looks at Jesus and then at Peter. The people are quiet now as they see tears pour down Peter's face. None of them has the heart to accuse him again. They know the truth. They also know this man is accusing himself more vehemently than they had done.

Jesus has eyes full of pity for Peter, and this is more than the disciple can bear. Peter runs out. He pushes through the gate, sobbing loudly as he tries to disappear from the world and from the loving scrutiny of Jesus's eyes (Luke 22:60–62).

8. Where do you think Peter is going and what do you imagine he might do?

9. **Step out of Scripture and back to today for this question. This is a two-part question.** *This is intended for reflection and need not be answered in a group.*

   Have you ever done something you wish you could turn back time to change? What would you like to tell Jesus now as he looks with compassion into your heart?

SELF-DELUSION

I am brave like Peter in battle
Until confronted with my own fears.
Denial comes before the rooster crows.
Then come tears.

LESSON 7

SIX TRIALS

MATTHEW 27:1–26; MARK 14:53–65, 15:1–20;
LUKE 23:1–25; JOHN 18:12–13, 19:1–16

Note

Six trials, including interrogations or hearings, are recorded in Scripture:

1. The interrogation before Annas, the previous high priest (John 18:12–13).

2. The interrogation before Caiaphas, high priest for that year (Luke 22:54).

3. The trial before Caiaphas and the council of the Sanhedrin (Matthew 26:57–68; 27:1; Mark 14:53–65; 15:1; Luke 22:63–71).

4. The initial hearing before Pilate (Luke 23:1–7).

5. The trial before Herod (Luke 23:6–12).

6. The trial before Pilate (Matthew 27:11–31; Mark 15:1–20; Luke 23:13–25; John 18:28–19:16).

1. What reasons, connected to a plot, do you think Caiaphas has for conducting the interrogation or preliminary hearing before dawn and then trying this case at daybreak (John 11:41–53; Matthew 27:1; Mark 14:55)? How long do you estimate you have been outside, waiting for Jesus's trial by the Sanhedrin to be finished? (You have been holding vigil since his arrest last night.)

Note

A Jewish document, the Mishnah, though not written until around AD 170, recorded the oral traditions concerning the rules that had been used for centuries in Jewish laws and courts. These would most certainly have pertained to cases like that of Jesus. The section on the Sanhedrin describes the guidelines that governed the Jewish council when it presided over a trial of an accused facing a possible death sentence.[1]

These are some of the procedures expected and the behaviors prohibited in a lawful trial by the Sanhedrin:[2]

Jewish law: Attempting to make the accused testify against himself, striking the accused during a trial, using only circumstantial evidence for a conviction, failing to have two witnesses agree, allowing conviction and sentencing for a capital offense to take place on the same day, and barring a public trial were all illegalities.

Jewish laws regarding questioning during a trial: The high priest was not to question the prisoner. However, witnesses for the prosecution were to be questioned and cross-examined extensively.

Jewish law regarding the Sanhedrin council: All trials were to be held in the hall of judgment in the temple area. Someone was required to speak on behalf of the accused. All Sanhedrin judges could argue for acquittal, but not all could argue for conviction. Capital cases were to follow a strict order, with arguments for the defense preceding arguments for conviction. The Sanhedrin judges were to hear a case and to discuss it in pairs all night before reconvening the next day to decide on a verdict and to impose sentencing. Trials were not to occur on the eve of the Sabbath or during festivals.

2. Is this a fair trial in your opinion (Matthew 26:59–60, 27:1; Mark 14:55–65)?

3. What is wrong with the testimonies of the so-called witnesses? (Compare Mark 14:55–61 with John 2:19-21.)

4. If you had testified for Jesus, what would you have said after having served close beside him every day? Did any of the disciples offer to be witnesses for Jesus?

5. **Step out of Scripture and back to today for this question.** If you were asked to be a witness, what personal knowledge would you share concerning the truth about Jesus?

6. Jesus is silent as most of the accusations are made. Why do you think he doesn't answer them

(Matthew 26:59–62)? How is this a fulfillment of prophecy (Isaiah 53:7)?

7. This is a four-part question. What has the high priest asked that Jesus is now answering (Matthew 26:63–64; Mark 14:60–62)? Is Jesus replying quietly or boldly? Why do you think he chose to answer this question (Daniel 7:13–14)? Who is the great I AM in the Mark passage? Compare this with Exodus 3:13–15 and John 14:6–10 to find your answer.

8. Where are the religious authorities taking Jesus to be tried next, and what time of day is it (Mark 15:1)?

9. What question does Jesus answer at his preliminary hearing with the governor, Pilate, so the Roman will know the gravity of what he is about to do (Luke 23:3–4)?

10. Where is Pilate sending Jesus next (Luke 23:4–7)?

11. You and John are waiting outside for a glimpse of Jesus and for any word about his trial before Herod. Friends of John from the high priest's household find you both and share the shocking news that Judas has hanged himself. Then they give you information only someone in the high priest's circle could know. What are you learning for the first time (Matthew 26:14, 27:3–5)? What prophecies in Scripture do you recall having heard read at the synagogue (Psalm 41:9; Zechariah 11:12–13)? How do you feel about this news?

12. Describe Herod's attitude when he meets Jesus (Luke 23:8–12). What prophecy is fulfilled by Jesus's silence (Isaiah 53:7–8)?

13. Herod sends Jesus back to Pilate. How do Pilate and his soldiers treat Jesus (Matthew 27:27–30)?

14. Pilate, who is a Roman and not a Jew, may have little knowledge of scriptural prophecies that point to Jesus as the Messiah. How does Jesus, exhausted and in pain, nevertheless make the effort to give Pilate some understanding of the truth (John 18:31–37, 19:11)?

15. What question does Pilate ask the King of the universe before turning away without listening for the answer (John 18:37–38)?

16. A message is delivered to Pilate. Outside, people are whispering gossip to one another about it. What do you overhear that gives you hope the governor could still release Jesus (Matthew 27:19)?

Scene

You are assessing the likelihood that Pilate will give Jesus an acquittal. You suspect the governor would like to free him just to spite the religious rulers, who have made Pilate's life so miserable since he was given his post here. On the other hand, you realize Pilate is keenly aware that because of his past miscalculations and blunders, his remaining prefect of Judea is tenuous. This makes you fear he will cave in to pressure from the religious leaders and the mob outside.

You recall the time Pilate attempted to impress his emperor by placing golden shields bearing Caesar's name in Herod's palace in the middle of the city. This enraged all the members of the Jewish community. They protested and finally appealed to Rome. Emperor Tiberius himself ordered the removal of the shields.[3]

That blemish on Pontius Pilate's record, along with other poor decisions, has brought his reputation to a low point in Rome. His shrewdness in dealing with the demands of the Jews (for whom he has great disdain) could possibly salvage his career.

Note

Contemporaries like Philo of Alexandria and Josephus describe Pontius Pilate as an extortionist, a tyrant, a blood-sucker, and a corruptible character. In his book *The Bible as History*, Werner Keller writes of Pilate, "He was cruel and his hard heart knew no compassion. His day in Judea was a reign of bribery and violence, oppression, misery, executions without fair trial and infinite cruelty."[4]

17. What horrible action is Pilate taking to appease this crowd (John 19:1)? How does the governor try to escape his responsibility as judge? (See any of these passages: Matthew 27:15–18, 20–23; Luke 23:13–22; John 19:5–15.)

Scene

You finally see Jesus standing above you on the platform. His eyes are swollen shut from blows he has received. He appears weak, swaying as he attempts to stay on his feet. Blood is running down his face. He has deep gashes from a wreath of thorns pressed into his scalp and forehead as a mock crown. His weary body is draped in a purple robe.

As Pilate asks which prisoner the mob wants released, your eyes scan the crowd. You recognize no one except for the chief priests, who urge the crowd to scream for Barabbas (Matthew 27:20; Mark 15:11; Luke 23:23).

18. What does the crowd shout that intimidates Pilate, causing him to wash his hands of the whole matter (John 19:12)?

19. You and your friends believe Pontius Pilate, as judge, has an opportunity to deliver justice in possibly the most important case he will ever hear. What is he doing instead (Matthew 27:23-26)?

20. **Step out of Scripture and back to today for this question.** Was Jesus the victim or the victor? Was he a martyr or a Savior? (This may be the most significant question in our study. Try to read all of these passages before answering: John 1:9–14, 3:16–17; Romans 5:6–8; Philippians 2:6–8; Hebrews 12:2–3.)

TRIAL

Lord, you washed the disciples' feet,
Even the feet that ran to betray.
Pilate, whose conscience would not be clean,
Washed his hands of you today.

LESSON 8

CRUCIFIXION

MATTHEW 27:32–56; MARK 15:21–41; LUKE
23:26–49; JOHN 19:16-37; ISAIAH 53

Note

*Some of the following information is graphic in
dealing with crucifixion. Parents may want to read
the Notes and Scenes (especially on pages 73-75) in
Lesson 8 first before deciding whether to summarize
that section for young children.*

Crucifixion was one of the most dreaded forms
of capital punishment in the Roman world. In fact,
this sentence was considered so abhorrent that
Rome made it illegal to flog or crucify any Roman
citizen, though some governors disregarded this law.
Floggings were done with a whip studded with bone
and metal. This tore deep into the flesh. Many died
from flogging.[1]

The prisoner was made to carry the cross on his
back to the place of execution. Cicero described
crucifixion as "the most cruel and frightful means

of execution." The Jewish historian Josephus called crucifixion "the most pitiable of all forms of death."[2]

Scene

Jesus is forced to carry his cross on a back, which has been torn by floggings. Finally, when Jesus can go no farther, a man from the crowd is forced to finish carrying the cross to Golgotha, the name of the hill just outside of Jerusalem where Jesus will be crucified. (Note: Golgotha means "the skull" in Aramaic and "Calvary" in Latin.)

You have seen crucifixions before, so you know Jesus's joints will gradually be pulled apart the longer he is on the cross. He will keep pushing against the cross, trying to stand on the thick nails lodged in his feet in order to stay upright. Otherwise his lungs will collapse under the hanging weight of his body, suffocating him.

This is the most unimaginable horror. Crucifixion is usually a long and painful death. Seeing the crucifixion of others has always been difficult, but watching this happen to your friend is heart-wrenching.

Jesus, whom you love, appears helpless. The hands that once touched and healed the sick and the hopeless are trembling now. His arms, forcibly stretched out against a wooden crossbeam, had not long ago gathered little children to sit beside him as he taught the crowds and his disciples.

You ate with Jesus by campfires and in people's homes, listening and learning from his wise counsel. You also watched in the temple as he confronted the most powerful religious rulers in the land. You know he is brilliant, kind, and endowed with amazing powers.

You were sure he was the Messiah. Today, his life and the life you have known and loved as you followed him are slowly ending. These are your final hours with your suffering Savior (Luke 23:49).

Note

In the suburbs of Jerusalem, archaeologists found the remains of a man named Yohanan ben Ha'galgol. A seven-inch spike was still lodged in his skeletal ankle with a fragment of olive wood attached. Scientists report he was crucified around the time of Jesus and was close to his age.[3]

For many years a debate continued over whether Jesus was tied to the cross with ropes or was impaled. Though ropes were frequently used to save the wood of the cross so it could be reused in subsequent crucifixions, this discovery provides evidence that nails were another means used to fasten a body to a cross. This was the case in Jesus's crucifixion, as accurately recorded in the Gospels.

1. Two other men are being crucified today, one on either side of Jesus. Which people continue to torment Jesus as he hangs on the cross (Matthew 27:38–44; Luke 23:35–39)? What are they saying?

2. Who stops ridiculing Jesus and becomes a believer? (For a sequence of events, compare Matthew 27:44 with Luke 23:39–43.) How can this criminal's repentance and belief in Jesus be proof that faith is enough for eternal salvation?

3. You are standing in the crowd. You look up at Jesus and then down at the soldiers, crouched on the ground, gambling for his outer robe. What prophecies are being fulfilled (Psalm 22:12–18; Isaiah 53)? List everything you see that is hurting your Lord Jesus.

4. What else is causing Jesus pain (Psalm 22:1–18; Matthew 27:37, 45–46; John 1:29)? How many hours is the sun blocked before Jesus calls out? As you stand in the darkness, what do you think is happening (Luke 23:44–46)?

5. List the acts of kindness and forgiveness Jesus shows others even as he suffers upon the cross (Luke 23:33–34, 42–43; John 19:25–27).

6. Which declarations from the cross cause you to believe Jesus knows the exact time of his death and knows he is going to be with his heavenly Father (Matthew 27:50; Luke 23:44–46; John 19:28–30)?

Scene

It is late afternoon now. You have been standing vigil close beside John, watching Jesus go through his agonizing death. Suddenly, you are startled by the loud sound of a forceful slam!

You feel a jolt, and the earth shifts back and forth beneath your feet. The ground begins to roll. The whole world seems to be moving (Matthew 27:50–54). You hear boulders split apart around you as Jesus calls out to heaven, "It is finished!" (John 19:30).

7. What do you think is happening or is going to happen?

8. Name some of the amazing and alarming events occurring in other places at that moment that you will later discover (Matthew 27:50–53).

Note

The thick veil, or curtain, in the temple separating the holy place from the Holy of Holies was torn at three in the afternoon. At that very moment Jesus spoke his last words and took his last breath, and the priests were presenting the evening sacrifice to God.

Shocked, the priests watched as the curtain was violently ripped from top to bottom before their eyes. In their book *Jesus on Trial*, Boice and Ryken point out the impact the tearing of the veil may have had on those priests. The authors suggest the result may be found in Acts 6:7: "So the word of God spread. The number of disciples in Jerusalem increased rapidly, and a large number of priests became obedient to the faith."[4]

Scene

The day looks like night as menacing clouds appear in the sky, threatening to unleash a storm. Beneath your feet the earth feels like it is ready to erupt. You and John struggle to keep from falling. You hear the rumbling sounds. As you look toward Jerusalem, you see the ground moving like a huge wave on the sea for miles.

The centurion stands beneath the cross of Jesus and notes the plaque, which says "King of the Jews," nailed above his head. This sign identifies the crime for which Jesus was sentenced. The soldier stares at the inscription. He tries to steady himself as the upheaval in the earth continues. He tilts his head to look up toward the face of Jesus and hears the Savior declare, "Father, into your hands I commit my spirit" (Luke 23:45–46).

You observed the centurion closely as he watched your teacher today. The Roman listened as Jesus spoke comforting words to his mother standing below him and gave hope to a crucified criminal on a cross beside him. The soldier looked surprised when Jesus asked his heavenly Father to forgive everyone—especially since the centurion, as the commanding officer, had ordered the nails to be hammered through Jesus's hands and feet.

Now Jesus's limp body hangs on the cross, which shakes and sways under a stormy sky. The ground slowly stops moving. Out of the blackness, sunlight breaks through dark clouds above Jesus's head.

Deliberately holding back emotion, the centurion proclaims, as if giving orders to all the other frightened soldiers, "Surely this was a righteous man! This was indeed the Son of God."

9. Who else, standing on that hill, proclaims Jesus to be the Son of God (Matthew 27:54; Mark 15:39; Luke 23:47)?

10. As you watch all this, do you think that the centurion was impressed by Jesus and is now a believer or that he was just frightened by the timing of the cataclysmic events?

11. **Step out of Scripture and back to today for this question. This is a three-part question.** What part of Jesus's crucifixion most impacted you? How did he show love that day and how does he show love now? Who do you proclaim Jesus to be?

FRIDAY

A horrible death on that terrible cross,
Then a quiet, darkened tomb.
No one could see through grief and loss
Resurrection was coming soon.

LESSON 9

LOVE AND LOSS

MATTHEW 27:55-66; MARK 15:42-47;
LUKE 23:50-56; JOHN 19:31-42

Note

Some of the additional information about the crucifixion is graphic in nature in the sections marked Notes and Scenes. Parents may want to read Lesson 9 first in deciding whether to summarize those sections for young children.

The death of Jesus is as important as his life. His critics charge he may not have died but could have fallen into a coma and come to his senses later in the tomb. This is known as the swoon theory.[1] So clear evidence of his death is imperative if his resurrection, which he promised, is to be believed.

Soldiers assigned to execute prisoners by crucifixion were experienced and proficient at their jobs and, by necessity, experts at pronouncing a prisoner dead. Pilate summoned the centurion to establish that Jesus of Nazareth was, in fact, dead (Mark 15:44–45). The centurion oversaw all the details of the crucifixion that day. He also had watched one of his soldiers thrust a spear into the dead prisoner's side. The body of Jesus was without reflex.

In his book *The Day Christ Died*, Jim Bishop puts forward the theory that when the soldier pushed his spear into the side of Jesus, he did so at such an upward slant that it pierced "the pleura and the thin part of the lung and stopped in the pericardium. The right auricle of the human heart holds liquid blood after death, and the outer sac holds the serum called the hydropericardium. When the soldier withdrew his spear, blood and water were seen to emerge and drip down the side of Jesus' body."[2] The executioners saw that Jesus was already dead. Thrusting the spear into his side was an afterthought (John 19:33–37).

Medical experts point to a possible cause of death: the heart of Jesus ruptured. The blood flowing into the pericardium, the lining around the wall of the heart, would have divided into a bloody clot and a watery serum. This would have become visible once Christ was pierced and blood and water came slowly from his side.[3]

The likely cause of death was asphyxiation. This happened when Jesus could no longer raise his chest, and his lungs therefore collapsed. Dehydration, infection and asphyxiation were how many of those crucified died.[4]

Crucifixion was a slow death, though Jesus died within a few hours and before those crucified with him. The religious rulers requested that all the crucified men have their legs broken and taken down from their crosses as the Sabbath was approaching (John 19:31–33).

To hasten death for the two criminals, their legs were broken so they could no longer use them to stand up and raise their chests to breathe; the two suffocated. This was Rome's cruel way of sending a lesson to anyone watching; capital punishment was not merely an execution but a painful experience to be avoided at all cost.

1. This is a three-part question. How can the spear thrust in Jesus's side and the soldiers' decision not to break his legs be fulfillment of prophecy? Besides the centurion and the soldiers, who witnesses these things? What two men take Jesus's dead body down from the cross? The answers to these questions can be found in Psalm 34:20, Zechariah 12:10, Mark 15:45–46, and John 19:30–37.

2. How does Joseph of Arimathea show devotion to Jesus even after his crucifixion (John 19:38–42)?

Do you think it takes courage for Joseph to approach Pilate for the body of Jesus (Matthew 27:57–60; Luke 23:50–54)?

3. As you follow the burial party, you are struck by the feeling you have seen Joseph of Arimathea before. You think you saw him walking briskly past you in the courtyard and into the Sanhedrin council meeting as it was finishing. Apparently the other religious rulers did not inform him of the trial and did not want his vote, though he is a member of the council. Why would they not want his vote (Mark 15:43–46)? What was the vote (Matthew 27:1–2; Mark 15:1; Luke 22:2, 71; 23:1–2)?

4. What do you know about Joseph of Arimathea (Matthew 27:57-60; Isaiah 53:9; Luke 23:50-51; John 19:38).

5. Who is the other man, Nicodemus (John 3:1–21, 7:50–51, 19:38–42)? You don't recall him participating in the Sanhedrin council meeting either.

6. How are they preparing Jesus's body for burial until the Sabbath is past (John 19:39–42)? What prophecy is being fulfilled (Isaiah 53:9)?

7. You look over your shoulder. Who else besides you is following to see where Jesus is being laid (Matthew 27:60–61)? Are these people risking arrest?

8. Are you concerned someone might arrest you?

9. What is the biggest worry of the Pharisees (Matthew 27:62–66)? Are they right to be concerned? (Note: Luke 24:9–12 is evidence of the disciples' frame of mind.)

10. You decide not to go home to your family, afraid your relatives might be arrested if the authorities find you there. You are unsure what is happening in the city right now. Finding the other disciples, you meet with them behind closed doors. Soldiers are combing the streets. What is your biggest concern as you talk with the other disciples?

11. List immediate and realistic fears you have today— for example, fear of arrest and crucifixion, fear for your family's safety, fear of being called naïve, or worse, a fraud.)

12. Amid all the chaos, you are grieving over the death of your teacher and close friend. List the losses you feel from the death of Jesus—for example, loss of a leader, loss of a friend, loss of direction, or loss of dreams. For ideas, see Mark 1:16–20 and John 1:41, 49–50, 6:2, 67–68, and 15:15–16.

13. **Step out of Scripture and back to today for this question. This is a two-part question.** What loss are you dealing with today? When fear and sadness threaten to overwhelm you, which comforting words of Jesus do you remember?

SATURDAY

When hope is gone,
Replaced by doubt and sorrow,
Tears blur any vision
Of an empty tomb tomorrow.

SUNDAY RESURRECTION

MATTHEW 28, MARK 16, LUKE 24, JOHN 20

Note

As you study this final and most exciting lesson, you may imagine yourself in each of the following settings with these people: Sunday morning with the women being greeted by angels, Sunday morning running with Peter and John to examine an empty tomb, Sunday afternoon traveling with friends and an unknown Scripture scholar on the road to Emmaus, and the evening of the first Easter sitting with the resurrected Jesus and the disciples.

This and every future Easter Sunday may take on a whole new meaning as you move through the day, looking for your risen Savior!

Scene

The dawn is breaking. The night fades and a yellow glow outlines the tops of buildings, reflecting off of the golden bricks of the temple in Jerusalem. Today is Sunday.

The hills are usually dry and rocky, but this morning they are covered in patches of soft green grass, speckled with yellow daisies and bright orange and purple flowers.[1] The daybreak paints the sky blue with ribbons of pink clouds.

This is a chilly but beautiful spring morning. You are walking with Mary Magdalene and the other women toward the tomb of Jesus. You are coming from Bethany to Jerusalem, so the journey began in the dark. Everyone is carrying spices and oils to anoint the Lord's body. You are all talking about the two earthquakes.

The first earthquake came on Friday as Jesus took his last breath on the cross. You and the women discuss all that has happened over these last three days and wonder about rumors you have heard. For instance, the tombs of many godly men and women are reported to have broken open as a result of the first quake (Matthew 27:51–53).

Some of your neighbors, who happened to be at the temple at the time of Jesus's death, told a fascinating story about the heavy curtain that hid the Holy of Holies there. The Holy of Holies is a room only the high priest is allowed to enter and only on the Day of Atonement to sprinkle the blood of the sacrifice on the mercy seat (Hebrews 9).

The curtain was torn from top to bottom right around the time of the sacrifice, just as Jesus was dying on the cross (Mark 15:38). Now anyone for the first time could access that holy place in the temple (Hebrews 10:19–23). How could an earthquake tear that thick, heavy cloth? Why would the curtain not simply have hung from its four hooks and four pillars (Exodus 26:31–34), swaying with the shifting earth? Was this the work of God during the crucifixion? If the curtain was indeed torn from top to bottom, who but the almighty Yahweh could have done this?

Today, a second earthquake just before sunrise woke people from their sleep. It toppled vases off of shelves. You and the others wonder what else happened as a result of this most recent earthquake (Matthew 27: 53).

What Mary, you, and your friends could not know was that a short time ago, following the second earthquake, an angel of the Lord appeared before a band of Romans soldiers.

The soldiers were to carefully guard the sealed tomb of Jesus. (Note: It is likely that a seal made of wax or clay was placed on a rope, which was wrapped around the giant stone that stood blocking the entrance to the tomb. No one could tamper with the tomb without breaking the seal.[2])

The armed men standing watch outside the tomb were astonished when a bolt of lightning struck near them and quickly morphed into the form of an angel (Matthew 28:2–4).

The celestial being rolled back the heavy stone from the tomb. The angel's clothes flashed and radiated a penetrating, iridescent light. The luminescent being lit the inside of the tomb.

The pulsing light confused and shocked the soldiers. They stood trembling with fear; some fainted (Matthew 28:4). They did not know what the supernatural being might do to them. To their surprise, he simply sat in the empty tomb, showing Jesus was already gone!

When the panic-stricken soldiers finally got on their feet, they pushed past one another, running as fast as they could. They found the religious rulers to whom Pilate had assigned them and recounted the fantastic events they had just witnessed. The chief priests and elders hastily assembled to find a way to discredit the story.

The soldiers were paid a large amount of money to tell a fabricated tale. They were to say that while they were asleep at their post, followers of Jesus stole the body.

The soldiers knew losing a charge assigned to them could be a death sentence, especially if they slept on guard duty. They also wondered how people could possibly believe sleeping men would know the disciples took the body. It seemed a ludicrous story. But the officials promised they would satisfy the governor if there were any questions. Confident the calculating old men would pay a big enough bribe to Pilate, the guards did as they were told. However, not everyone would tell the lie or keep the secret (Matthew 28:11–15).

Note

As the story develops, keep some of these facts in mind. Mary Magdalene seems to be singled out as a prominent figure among the believing women just as Peter is still portrayed as the leader of the disciples. Different gospels provide additional and varying facts.

You will notice some divergence among gospel accounts. Matthew and Mark, for instance, have one angel at the tomb, while Luke and John have two. The Gospels also differ over the sequence of events and the names of women, though they all have Mary Magdalene arriving at the tomb. In the gospel of John, Mary Magdalene is the only woman mentioned, and yet when she tells Peter and John (described as "the other disciple") about the empty tomb, she says, "They have taken the Lord's body and *we* don't know where they have put him" (John 20:2). By combining all the Gospels, we see a more complete picture of Sunday's remarkable events!

1. The sun is sliding out from behind the early morning clouds. You and the women near the burial place of Jesus. As you walk through the garden, someone asks, "Who is going to move that heavy stone?" Before anyone decides what to do, you arrive at the tomb. Each of you stops and stares at the huge stone, which has been rolled back, exposing the entrance. The grave is open and the room is empty! What do you assume has happened?

Scene

Mary turns abruptly and runs into the city. She intends to find Peter and John to tell them about the empty tomb (John 20:1–11). (Note: The two men had stood watch in the courtyard during the trials in Jerusalem. John was at the crucifixion on the hill outside of Jerusalem. They apparently never left the city. They appear to be staying together, possibly at a separate house from the other disciples.) Mary knows exactly where to find them (John 20:2).

You and the remaining women encounter an angel at the tomb who shares the exciting news that Jesus has risen from the dead (Matthew 28:5–6)!

[Note: Mark is the only gospel writer recording that the women were so frightened they told no one what they had seen. Mark may have meant the women were so frightened they told no one they passed in the streets as they ran to tell the disciples the news (Mark 16:5–8).] You and the women run to the house in Bethany where the other disciples are staying (and where Jesus and the twelve often stayed). You share with the men all you saw and heard at the tomb (Matthew 28:7–8).

Mary's announcement of an empty tomb sends Peter, John, and you running to see for yourselves. John and you reach the tomb first, stopping at the threshold. He leans inside to see the linen grave clothes neatly folded (John 20:3–10). You wonder, *Why would someone bother to remove the grave clothes and then place them back on the grave shelf? Why not just take the body wrapped?* Peter arrives and bolts into the empty room.

2. Will you enter or stay outside the tomb? Why or why not?

3. John now steps inside. You notice John looks as if he remembers something (Matthew 20:17–19). What words of Jesus do you recall even though you might not completely understand them?

4. Peter and John leave the tomb to return to where they were staying. As you see the expressions on their faces, what do you suspect is changing in the mind and the heart of one of these men (John 20:8–10)?

Scene

As Peter and John silently walk away from the empty tomb, Mary Magdalene arrives. Overwhelmed with grief and sobbing, Mary is alone with no answers. As she bends over and looks inside the tomb, she sees two angels in white seated where the body of Jesus had been, one at the head and the other at the foot (John 20:11–12).

The angels ask her, "Woman, why are you crying?" Mary does not realize she is speaking to angels as she weeps, her face buried in her hands. (Note: In the Bible, angels appearing as messengers typically looked like men. Angels were sometimes surrounded with an aura of bright light, as witnessed by the soldiers. The angels who spoke to Mary wore white robes but did not have any apparent illumination.)

Mary is on a mission to find Jesus. She cannot perform a last act of love by anointing his body. She explains she is so distraught, "Because they have taken away my Lord, and I don't know where they have taken him" (John 20:11–13).

Mary turns and sees a blurry figure through her tears. She sobs even harder. Thinking he is the gardener, she irrationally imagines that if he has moved the body, she can carry it back to the tomb. Her grief intensifies as she begs him to tell her where he has laid Jesus (John 20:14–16).

5. What does Jesus say to help Mary recognize him (John 20:16)? What does he tell her not to do, which may help her realize the change needed in their relationship (John 20:17)?

6. Mary Magdalene hurries off to tell the disciples of Christ's resurrection (John 20:18). Jesus now greets the other women and you on the road. All of you fall at his feet and grab him around the ankles. Why do you imagine Jesus allows this when he had told Mary Magdalene not to cling to him (Matthew 28:8–10)?

7. How is Mary Magdalene's confusion and sadness turning to boldness and certainty (John 20:18)?

8. Do the disciples believe Mary Magdalene, the other women, or you after hearing about your encounters with angels and with the risen Christ (Mark 16:9–11; Luke 24:9–11)? Why not? How does that make you feel?

9. **Step out of Scripture and back to today for this question. This is a three-part question.** Can you recall a miracle Jesus has done in your life that might be hard for others to believe? What evidence and eyewitnesses from these passages confirm to you Jesus is alive? If you doubt the resurrection of Jesus, how do you feel after learning even his close disciples doubted he could or would rise from the dead?

Scene

This is Sunday afternoon. You are walking with two men, friends of yours. One is Cleopas. Like you, they had followed Jesus since the beginning of his ministry. You are on the road to Emmaus, anxious to leave Jerusalem behind. You and your friends are heartsick. Shaking your heads, you discuss the recent crucifixion of your beloved teacher. You can't believe that he is gone or that his end would come in this way.

A stranger appears and walks with you and your friends. He asks questions about your conversation (Luke 24:13–32). You can hardly believe he is coming from Jerusalem and has not heard of the travesty of justice that Pilate carried out at the request of the religious rulers. Your rabbi was the most beloved, righteous, and amazing man of recent times. He was the future and the hope of your people. Now he is gone and so is your hope.

You are frustrated and still in disbelief. You give the stranger details about the last few days. With some embarrassment, you share the outrageous story the women told after returning from an empty tomb this morning.

To your astonishment, the man explains why these events had to take place. He refers to Moses and the prophets. He interprets Scripture passages you know but never understood until now. With every prophecy the stranger quotes, the life and death of Jesus seem more intentional and meaningful. You can ask this man nothing for which he does not have a compelling answer.

The seven miles spent traveling to Emmaus seem to pass in minutes as your sorrow dissolves into excitement. An empty tomb is quickly becoming a promise! You are fascinated and for the first time comforted. You and your friends beg the man not to leave.

The sun is setting as you arrive in the little village of Emmaus. Together you convince your new teacher to stay for a meal. You want to hear more from him.

The stranger sits down with you and breaks a piece of bread in two. He then looks to heaven and prays aloud. You look at your new friend intently, listening as he gives thanks. His voice sounds very familiar now. You have heard him pray over many meals with you, including a miraculous feeding of five thousand people with a few fish and loaves of bread (Matthew 14:18–19)?

The man hands each of you a piece of bread. You are startled to see his face is no longer that of a stranger. The others seem to recognize him too. You are, each one, astounded by your discovery. You and your friends have the same surprised expression on your faces. At that moment, *Jesus* disappears!

10. Why do you think you did not recognize this roadside scholar was Jesus until he sat down to break bread and pray?

11. Where are you and your friends going after this encounter (Luke 24:32–35)? Note: You have just heard some disturbing news on the streets, though it is somewhat less alarming now that you have been with the risen Christ. The rumor is quickly

spreading that the body of Jesus was stolen. Chief priests have named all of you as grave robbers (Matthew 28:12–13)!

12. Who had a private audience with the risen Christ (Luke 24:34; 1 Corinthians 15:5)? What do you imagine Peter and Christ talked about in their moments together?

13. As you and your friends are gathered together, who appears in the room? How does he help you realize you are not seeing an apparition (Luke 24:36–43)? (Note: In his book *Addresses on the Gospel of John*, H. A. Ironside has pointed out that after his resurrection Jesus was able to present his body in flesh and bone. But as he was no longer subject to former laws, he entered a room without coming through a doorway. As Ironside so aptly put it, "He no longer self-limited himself!"[3])

14. This three-part question relates to this evening with your risen Savior. How do you feel as you watch Jesus eat and listen to him speak (Luke 24:44–49)? Do you wish he would stay, or can you believe he is with you whether you see him or not? List the questions you want to ask him. You are not yet ready for Jesus to leave! As he disappears in front of your eyes, a single question fills your mind, *"What happens now?"*

15. **Step out of Scripture and back to today for these final questions.** Has stepping into Scripture made these events more real or meaningful to you? How? Give examples.

16. What did you discover or rediscover stepping into Scripture, Seder to Sunday?

17. If you have never asked Jesus to be your personal Savior, is that something you would like to do now that you have taken a few steps closer to him in Scripture? If you already enjoy that relationship, are you ready to step even closer as you study the Bible more deeply and talk with Jesus more often each day? If you answer yes to either of these questions, write your new commitment in the space below, and then date it so you have a record for yourself whenever you want to look at it.

My new
Commitment

_____

_____

Date

YOUR TOMB/MY TOMB

Lord Jesus,
Before you came into my heart,
My life was like your tomb,
Practical, useful, utilitarian,
But always that chill of gloom.

Hewing it from the rock had a purpose,
And though the purpose had an end,
No goals or the best intentions
Could stop fears from sealing me in.

Then I cried, "Be my Savior, Lord Jesus,"
And the dark grew as light as the day.
I walked out to a life of such joy with you,
I had not noticed the stone rolled away.

Seder to Sunday: Step into Scripture, a Bible Study for Easter is the first in the *Step into Scripture* Bible study series. If you have enjoyed this study and want to order more, or wish to have other Bible studies in the series as they become available, contact me at www.sedertosunday.com or check your local bookstore or Christian book sellers.

Writing this study and including you in scenes from biblical history was a joy and a labor of love. I thank you for choosing to take this journey into Scripture using *Seder to Sunday* as your time machine. God bless you. And I hope all of your Easter Sundays are more meaningful because you were there.

ACKNOWLEDGMENTS

I thank the people who tried this study when it was still in the early stages and had only a vague resemblance to the finished product. They did this before I decided to make *Seder to Sunday* part of a larger *Step into Scripture* Bible series. These kind people were adventurous and curious and were willing to try something different.

I am grateful to Cathy and Dick Ferris, who first provided this Bible study, then under development, to people in their church in Bakersfield, California, and to others wanting a personal Bible study for the Easter season.

I am thankful to our late, beloved Pastor Dale Paulsen, who took a chance on me, and to the wonderful people in our group at Morro Bay Presbyterian Church who joined me in the first Seder to Sunday Bible Study.

I offer a big thank-you to Sandy and Brian Rehkopf for using *Seder to Sunday* in their church in Bakersfield. I am grateful to members of their Sunday school class for taking this study with them on their camping retreat and for passing it on to others. Again, they were courageous enough to undertake this study when it was still in its rough draft.

A heartfelt thank-you to my husband, Jerry, who created the map in this book and who listens and advises. He is my best critic and my greatest supporter. His faith in me and his belief in the need for this type of interactive study kept me writing.

I am grateful to the Lord for giving me the idea. His close guidance kept me navigating through the Gospels. I needed to handle his Word carefully while piecing together a picture people could enter with their hearts and imaginations.

I am most thankful that God's Word became flesh and blood when Jesus Christ came among us so long ago. How wonderful that as we all step into Scripture, we can experience a closer relationship with the One who stepped into this world for us.

NOTES

All Scripture citations, unless otherwise specified, are taken from the *New International Bible* (Grand Rapids: Zondervan Publishing House, 1995). NKJV refers to the *New King James Version* (Nashville: Thomas Nelson Inc., 1982).

Lesson 1

1. *Filming in Israel*, "The Original Biblical Palm Trees," Biblical Productions, www.biblicalproductions.com.document.
2. John MacArthur, *The MacArthur New Testament Commentary* (Chicago: Moody Bible Institute, 1988), 268.
3. C. F. Cruse, *Eusebius' Ecclesiastical History* (Peabody, MA: Hendrickson), 26.
4. Flavius Josephus, *Josephus: Complete Works*, trans. William Whiston (Grand Rapids, MI: Kregel Publishing, 1985), 379.
5. Ceil and Moshi Rosen, *Christ in the Passover* (Chicago: Moody Publishers, 2006), 69.

Lesson 2

1. John F. Walvoord and Roy B. Zuck, eds., *Dallas Theological Seminary, The Bible Knowledge Commentary: An Exposition of the Scriptures* (Wheaton, IL: Victor, 1983), vol. 2:321.

Lesson 3

1. Walvoord and Zuck, eds., *The Bible Knowledge Commentary:* vol. 2: 320.

Lesson 5

1. John F. Walvoord, *Matthew: Thy Kingdom Come* (Chicago: Moody, 1982), 221.

Lesson 6

1. F. B. Meyer, *F. B. Meyer Bible Commentary* (Wheaton, IL: Tyndale House, 1979), 475.
2. Walvoord and Zuck, *The Bible Knowledge Commentary*, vol.2: 210.
3. Charles R. Swindoll, *The Greatest Life of All, Jesus* (Nashville: Thomas Nelson, 2008), 191–92.
4. F. F. Bruce, *New Testament History.* (New York: Double Day, 1969), 64.
5. Werner Keller, *The Bible as History* (New York: Bantam Books, 1982), 283–84.
6. Charles F. Pfeiffer and Everett F. Harrison, *The Wycliffe Bible Commentary* (Nashville: Moody, 1968), 980.
7. Randall Price, *The Stones Cry Out: What Archaeology Reveals About the Bible* (Eugene, OR: Harvest House, 1997), 305.
8. Laurna L. Berg, "The Illegalities of Jesus' Religious and Civil Trials," *Bibliotheca Sacra*, vol. 161, no. 643 (July-September 2004): 331, http://www.christianitytoday.com/ct/1998/april16/jesus-v-sanhedrin.html.

Lesson 7

1. Jesus v, Sanhedrin, Darrell L. Boch, April 6, 1998, http://www.christianitytoday.com/ct/1998april6/jesus-v-sanhedrin.html
2. Berg, "The Illegalities of Jesus' Religious and Civil Trials," 330–35.
3. Keller, *The Bible as History*, 385.
4. Ibid.

Lesson 8

1. James Montgomery Boice and Philip Graham Ryken, *Jesus on Trial* (Wheaton, IL: Crossways Books, 2002), 80.
2. Keller, *The Bible as History*, 387.
3. Price, *The Stones Cry Out*, 309–10.
4. Boice and Ryken, *Jesus on Trial*, 109.

Lesson 9

1. Swindoll, *The Greatest Life of All*, 233.
2. Jim Bishop, *The Day Christ Died* (New York: Harper Collins, 1977), 257.
3. Henry H. Halley, *Halley's Bible Handbook: An Abbreviated Bible Commentary* (Minneapolis: Zondervan, 1962), 449.
4. "This Bone is the Only Skeletal Evidence in the Ancient World," *Kristina Killgrove, forbes.com* July 20, 2018. https://www.forbes.com/sites/kristenakillgrove/2015/12/08/this-bone-provides-the-only-skeletal-evidence-for-crucifixion-in-the-ancient-world/

Lesson 10

1. "Jerusalem's Month of Flowers," *People.fas.harvard.edu.,* Aug. 23, 2018.
2. Pfeiffer and Harrison, *Wycliffe Bible Commentary,* 984.
3. H. A. Ironside, *Addresses on the Gospel of John* (Neptune, New Jersey: Loizeaux Brothers, Inc., 1984), 868.

The map was drawn by Jerry L. Boyd specifically for this Bible study. Portions of the map were inspired by the following maps:

"Map of the Last Passover and the Death of Jesus," *Bible History Online* > *map_jesus* > *MAP.*

"The Road to Calvary," Jesus-story.net., www.jesus-story.net > map_calvary_route.

"Jerusalem in Jesus' Time," *NIV Bible* (Grand Rapids: Zondervan, 1984), Map 8.